A
MOON
MADE
OF
COPPER

A Moon Made of Copper© Chris Bose, 2014

Published by Kegedonce Press
11 Park Road
Neyaashiinigmiing, Ontario N0H 2T0
www.kegedonce.com
Administration Office/Book Orders

RR7 Owen Sound, ON N4K 6V5

Printed in Canada
Cover Art: Bracken Hanuse Corlett
Design: Eric Abram
Author photo: Nicki Mackenzie

Library and Archives Canada Cataloguing in Publication

Bose, Chris, author
  A moon made of copper / Chris Bose ; edited by Joanne Arnott.

Poems.
ISBN 978-0-9868740-8-6 (pbk.)

  I. Arnott, Joanne, 1960-, editor II. Title.

PS8553.O7372M66 2014   C811'.54   C2014-904316-3

Sales and Distribution - http://www.lpg.ca/LitDistco:
For Customer Service/Orders
Tel 1-800-591-6250 Fax 1-800-591-6251
100 Armstrong Ave. Georgetown, ON L7G 5S4
Email orders@litdistco.ca

We acknowledge the support of the Canada Council for the Arts which last year invested
$20.1 million in writing and publishing throughout Canada.

We would like to acknowledge funding support from the Ontario Arts Council, an agency
of the Government of Ontario.

Dedicated to Mike Jules, aka MASK,
Skate on brother, R.I.P. 2014.

Table of Contents

Cycles of Death

The crow is at my lips

The Demon

The shh-ya-a and I

The flood and the fire are true

While you slept I ate the world

Cycles of Death

Dead words:

You stitched your name
across my mouth
told me to be quiet
'hush' you said
'the elders will hear you'
we were united
again and again in that tight knot
flesh of ecstasysweatcum
you moaned and gave me
that look I have seen
a thousand times
in your embrace

later that day your mother
called and said I was too old for you
I agreed and told her I would not disappear
she hung up I put down the phone
you emerged from the shower
crawled beneath the sheets
with me again
you nailed one hand to the bedpost
then the other
we vowed to see this to the end

Cycles of Death:

I saw dozens of elk cross the river
on a cold January morning
on my way to see you
The sky cracked open
light splashed across the sky
a thousand years of secrets

I told you everything
we built planes and dreamt of ways
to escape the small town of madness
before you succumbed
drank from the punch

I met your chief
I saw your mother
moving through the darkness
while deer crashed through the forest
branches snapping
like little thunder storms
in a giant womb

I had no idea it would end like this
a blue sky
green earth below me
I fell I did not close my eyes

She kills me:

Every night I close my eyes
praying I will leave
go across the country
to my woman's warm bed
inviting lips
promises of a new destiny

I try to drink myself to death
but my ex only laughs and throws knives at me
carving me up as I lay paralyzed by her venom
my children hopelessly tangled in her womb

I drive dangerously fast
often find myself on the edges of cliffs
tall buildings
staring down at the hard ground
feeling that magnetic pull of death

I curse myself for being a coward
bite my tongue until it bleeds
she sews her name across my chest
attaches skulls to my spine
telling me I am worthless
and I will die
in her arms

Death rattles:

I hear them at night
calling me like wolves
I crawl out of bed
step onto a floor of black widows
gently pick up a handful
wincing in pain as they bite
eating one after another
black bulbous sacks of poison exploding
red in my mouth

In the next room are piles of black scorpions
I feel them jab at my feet, it's like walking over
beds
of cactus
I feel tired
keep moving into the next room full of soft
pink worms

Here I collapse as scorpions crawl on my face
and worms
shudder beneath me
I can see out the window
one lonely star in the night sky
I feel a scorpion climb
into my mouth, it stabs away at my soft red flesh
everything fades to black
I crash crying out of some woman's womb
trapped to begin this deadly cycle again

If you fear dying:

A crow sews my eyes shut
while a cougar licks my arms and torso
a thick velvety tongue slurping against me
I pray that I can see her insane letters one more time

I will know it was all worth it
I wasn't wrong
I wasn't a coward

I lay my body down
in the soft dewy grass
feeling the sun bleach my rib bones
while coyotes tear at the flesh

I hear bears fucking in the distance
a full moon
a sharp knife
a decidedly dumb way to go

I can feel her move beneath me
the mother of all
pumping and pulsing
I grin a broken-jawed skeleton grin
laughing a silent laugh as crows peck at my eyes

A thousand years:

Underneath a night sky
I crash through the forest
panting panting
gasping to catch my breath
hearing something smash through the darkness behind me

I stumble up, not used to four legs
this weird sound comes out of my mouth
not a word,not a voice
a strange baying screech
my horns covered in fuzz
twelve points in the night
twelve blades towards the light

I charge across a field
beneath a full moon
hear dozens of feet behind me
closing in faster and faster
leathery pads thumping a mad drum beat
against our mother

I know I am not young any longer
my battles are fewer and fewer
blood glistens on my hind leg
shimmering as the sharp teeth gather around
glowing like my horns
I charge towards them all
smashing into the night

Death is a museum:

My body stares up at the lights
glowing as some guy tugs at the flesh
with a scalpel
we have never met
we have never talked
we never will reminisce about the past
or old hockey games
concerts or drunken stories
He just diligently cuts away
at my chest
breaks out the bone saw
while his hand moves across memories
a past
a lover's caress
a kiss
long forgotten
tube sucks out my blood
scoops my stomach
intestines, lungs and other organs
I stare down at my body
scream
I am not dead
He begins cutting open my skull
A light spills across the room

The sun is tangled
like death in black branches:

Crows dance on the wind
Ravens dance on the bones
I smell sagebrush and taste the dirt
handful upon handful
I fall off the cliff
towards a red earth
screaming every profanity I know
cursing everyone who has cut their names
across my chest and back
arms and legs
Flames erupt across the sky
I drink gasoline
waiting to explode
sitting at my desk
answering a phone and taking a message
Behind me a coyote laughs
a wheezing, gasping laugh
I cock a rifle
put it towards my right eye
pray that all I need is one good eye
to find my way through
the spiritworld

I, the Resurrector of the dead:

I cock the gun
put it into my mouth
sweat pours down my forehead
I think of a thousand different things
wonder if I'm doing the right thing
I know there is no other way
out of this situation
She calls my name from the bed
this distracts me
I should have known better

I think of flying
staring at the ground
from 36000 feet
sipping a beer and feeling it tingle
across my tongue

She calls my name again
I stretch my body like a hide
waiting to be tanned
under a hot sun
a sharp knife

I have fought countless wars
the medals are stitched
across my chest

Fuck Death:

I crawl from another womb
spitting out afterbirth and placenta
disgusted at this ritual over and over

I don't cry this time
the doctor shakes me
spanks me
I put my finger in my mouth, bored

He hands me to her
I suckle at a breast
trying to remember the last time I was here

All I know is this:

The gill net we used
when I was younger
used to catch salmon
it doesn't anymore
The land I grew up on
is poisoned
we cannot eat the game
or what we grow
or drink the water that flows
All I know is this:
The cleaver to the bone
is not only a tool for a butcher
but for a select few women
who know the path
clear and sharp to my heart
words also cut
into soft flesh
All I know is this:
I miss my children
by the minute
by the hour
I will never abandon them
the night is terrible
for that's when I miss them
the most

All I know is this:
love is you wretching
up your stomach
when you get dumped
praying for the bullet
to cure your aching heart
the headache that won't go away
All I know is this:
The bullfighter doesn't always win
Hemingway blew away his promise

my father cut my umbilical cord
and walked away
drowning his soul with a bottle

All I know is this:
Every street I walk down
I carve my name into the pavement
I scream at the buildings
my words bounce around the glass
and steel and concrete
losing my self a little bit every day

All I know is this:
The streets are filled
with beautiful temptations
you have to be aware
of the blade
the pills
the sacrifices people make

All I know is this

I am a moon made of copper:

Made of glass
I will know your dreams
I will eat your memories
I will devour your love
I will tear down the night
drive down your roads
past your homes
your sleeping families
your tender dreams
I will skin them like a cat
Put your chair against the door
the butcher knife on the counter
the pills by the water
I will wring you dry
like a wet rag
I am a moon made of copper
made of glass
made of war
crushing stones in my mouth
I will burn down your cities
I will love my woman
I will pay my lawyer
I will think about the small rooms
before the parasites
before I made you these promises
before I took it all back from you

The crow is at my lips

The illusionist:

The illusion is that
reading this poem
will bring you closer
to me
I won't win you back
you will not forgive

The wolves howling at night
are hungry for our blood
the stars falling
the earth shaking
the volcanoes erupting
spewing hot molten lava
will not heal our wounds

No
we will die alone
you will never forgive
the illusions I labour under
only make the dark
that much heavier
as the leaves
fall from the trees
so too will every
last secret I held from you

This is as real as it gets:

The cold sea wind on my face
The water crashing against the shore
The dark sky above
The tattered sails as we push towards land
The thunder booming loud and hungry
The beer and wine were green and lousy
I think back to shore leave and
The young deck hand
with some whore in his arms (strangely, she
looked like my ex)
as he worked it in and out
she moaned and her red hair tossed
and flowed
that smile on his face
that malice in his eyes
feral and hungry
I couldn't take it
I smashed everything
took a box of memories to mail back to you
The boat heaves
The hull groans
The captain is down
It's just me and the deck hand
I'll make sure only one of us
Makes it to shore

The honeymoon phase:

never lasts forever
by the fourth night you've worked it out
the sex thing
you've done it in the shower
standing up
on the sofa
the kitchen table
the washing machine
pumping away like mad
all night
filling her up with each taut
tenuous moment
you are about to blow like a great whale
that feeling rising up your spine
your eyes roll back in your head
her breath short and fast
sweat on your chest
her hands eagerly pulling on your ass
pushing you all the way inside as you groan
and moan and finally
just let go
filling her up
rolling off after a moment's pause or so
perhaps lighting up a smoke
finally you both start to talk
get to know each other

Pillow talk:

I know this well
when you are lying on your back
beside your new woman
or new man
blowing smoke towards the ceiling
gingerly touching one another
with feet
hands
caressing stroking
to reassure each other of the moment
of the intimacy, of the good
You are getting to know one another
becoming friends
bonding
She listens intently to your every word
nods in agreement or disagrees accordingly
He listens to her
smiling and nodding
but he's already thinking of the next round
pushing it down that tight wet hole
filling it up again
Don't fool yourself ladies
Men are beasts
we really often
only have one thing on our minds
especially when we already have you in bed

The crow is at my lips:

The snake is in my bones
The worms dig inside of me
The eyes were the first to go
Live with her a few months
You'll know the longest days of your life
Something was wrong with us
It was one thing after another
Disaster to disaster
It was like being in a drunken boat
Never knowing which way it was going
How long it would last this time
Before the next break up
Towards the end there she got good
Knives would unfurl from her tongue
Blades would sing by my head
She said I was just like my mother
She really knew how to hurt a guy
I ran for the door

The crow is at my lips
The snake inside my skull
I am a lonely night
Full of people wanting to die
Wanting to live
Wanting a way out
But not willing to work for it
I am the curse on her lips
The drag of her cigarette
The glimmer in her eyes
As he mounts her from behind
And slowly slips it inside her.

Two weeks:

into a romance
with a beautiful
young woman
nearly half my age
I wait for the spider
for the perfect things
like a tiger in the jungle
a boa constrictor at the edge
of a swamp

After all these years
I figure I finally met someone
I can get along with and not worry
or explain things to her
or worry if she can hold her booze
when we go out

Guys always hit on her
warn me not to leave her alone
but I know better
she is the spider
she is the tiger in the jungle
she is the boa constrictor
at the edge of the swamp

what they don't know is
I've waited a very long
time to find someone
like that

Rockets against the sky:

A bullet in my left ribcage
a knife follows it
followed by a fist
that punches through
all the way to my back
grabbing a fistful of
blood, bone and gristle
all this as I cough my lungs out

My kids demand
we go to the fair
the pool
the puppy store

I notice a jet stream
high above
I point it out
to momentarily
distract them
telling them it's a rocket
and that I was on one last week

somehow
this amazes them
and I'm able to climb
back up into the mountains
become a god again to them
even for just a few minutes

Outside the grey skies

are unrelenting
sunlight is unable to part the curtains
I wander around town
looking for messages
putting up bulletins
asking for help
walking around with a wound
that looks like a gunshot
past drunks
derelicts
rich and elite
madness clutching all of them
wondering where my daughter is
will she be able to forgive me

will she be able to forgive me
look into my eyes and tell me
"It's alright dad, you did your best
I don't care what mom says, I still love you."
one day
that's all I want to hear

when will the explosive night come
when I cannot run from the cold hard
facts of estrangement
the love of another woman

can I do it?

can I endure night after night
of intoxication
staring down the barrel of lust
knowing that each night I murder a part of her
a part of me
a part of our child

will we both bleed
when I drive the knife
between us

she hates me already
soon I must make it absolute
but not tonight
not after I finish this gin and tonic
after I listen to another song
from Leonard Cohen's dark underworld

not after I shower
or get a haircut
not on the phone
while I'm away
in another city
not looking into her eyes
night after night
not even remembering what colour
they are
after all these years

not after a walk through
the moonlit night
and especially not after
a bender

"Stop feeling guilty
for wanting to be happy"
is what a woman I've confided in has told me
and I want her (and if what they say is true)
she knows this as well

Me again

Hello there
It's me again
I come before you
   now
in   a vision
a nightmare
this is a warning
that everything is alright
I am not killing you
in your sleep
but I am coming

I will not be content
to stay in
 pemmican/salmon-soaked stories
in teepees
 wigwams
   winter-lodges
    and
longhouses

THIS MEANS WAR
and this means that
I will invade you
and
your life
I will come out of the square box in your living room
I will cut you scalp you gut you rip you leave you for dead and
make sinew from your intestines for my bows I will use your bones
for spear tips arrow heads
toothpicks
but relax
don't take this all so seriously

I am joking
I am the trickster
I come before you now
in the
shape of a coyote

consider yourself lucky
this time

I could come before
you
in the shape of a grizzly
maul you tear shred you
blood dripping from my carnivorous teeth
saliva red gore dripping from my mouth
but I won't

I'll just appear as a crow
to shit on your windshield after you finish
washing
and waxing your car

I will be the ants invading your house
the weeds you cannot kill in the driveway
a spider crawling up your legs under the
blankets as you sleep

I will be the owl
that shows up on your balcony
outside your door when you leave
warning you
 screeching at you ripping into your dreams

I want to scare
   you
  to death
 peck out your eyes while the paramedics arrive
to resuscitate you

so beware
I am coming
 I will
  take you
this is war

  these are the lines
this is how it will
end

there are no more nice NDN
stories

Deadman

I have been
into every
room
but this one

a room
full of scars
the scar
on the left side of my face
the ones in my eyes
the girl in my class with
the odd scar
on her throat
over the jugular

outside
the past is dead
leaves flicker
on trees
like
waves in
the moonlight
sunlight
whatever

" I could use a drink"
" what is the significance of the moon?"

The moon watches
all
of us
like a surrogate father
the night
our mother
embracing
each other and each
one of us
we all sleep alone

" Make it a double "
" I haven't drank in years "

In here
the past
is not dead

like a plane crash
a car wreck
a war zone
the past always intruding
in the present

" Drinks all around"

a scar is caused by the tissue
not being able
to heal properly

a child brandishing
a straight razor
releases
liquid into the
air of night
something special

" What's happening? "
 "something wonderful"
 "What do you remember?"
 " nothing. "

and you sleep again and again and again

" I remember... nothing "

See you there

Day Four / 6:42pm

The land is flat
in eastern montana
(I tell you this
in case you've never been there)
when a storm comes down
the sky can be clear blue to the east
dark and forbidding to the west

it was day four
after the feast
we were nearly the last to leave
we helped clean the arbour
it was absolutely
fucking miraculous

the sun had beaten down
hard on us for four days
as soon as it was over
as soon as the last dancer left the arbour
the sky grew dark
relief

Day Three / 4:54 am

waking on the third day
crawling out of the teepee
seeing the morning mist envelop the arbour
the teepees stretching for the clear   blue sky
the chill   of dawn
in the prairies

hearing my uncle laugh behind me
"you were still dancing in your sleep, nephew!"

Day Four / 7:39 pm

we met this one indian guy
from washington state
(I can't remember exactly from where)
whose ride had broken down
on a straight stretch of highway
where a car can look so small
so insignificant
so vulnerable
especially when a prairie storm
is coming down
all dark and purple like
bruises

we stopped because we knew him
we had just been through four days of sweat
blood and starvation with him
and before that   we had been with him
in bear butte
(I remember helping dig a pit for him, for his
four days on the mountain)
it would be a dishonour not to help him

He stood over the engine of his car
as it leaked precious
green life blood
from the radiator
he laughed
he told us not to worry
it was apparent
he was not supposed to leave that day
we all had a nervous laugh
went our separate ways

Bear Butte South Dakota: May 12/94

we were digging his pit
(which looked suspiciously like a grave)
into the side of bear butte
pick and shovel
pick and shovel
pick pick pick
through the limestone
the earth
the sweat
the ticks

letting someone else take over
sitting hypnotized   on the side of the
mountain

watching golden eagles swoop down
grabbing snatching gripping ripping
at rabbits and gophers

I was staring at the passage of time

he came over
pulled me back
told me about why we were digging a pit   how he got
his pipe his voice gentle his braids shining in the sun like
two black gun barrels sweat streaming down the sides of
his face

he had to be one tough
sonuvabitch
to sit it out like this
for four days and four nights
no food no water
in a pit roughly the same size as a grave

he told me some guys have done their fast in
waist deep water
days in the water

I sat there on the edge of the mountain
lulled into trance by clouds pouring over land-
scape
 sounds of the pick slamming
into the limestone of bear butte
holyland
for pilgrims
of the red road

I sat there on the side of the mountain
the silence of
the clouds blowing across the land
grazed my head
my mind
heart

in the distance
I could see devil's tower
yet

I heard something
someone
"come with us"
they said
"come with us"

The Demon

A pipeline to god:

In every needle
in every crack pipe
in every bottle
in every cigarette
in every city
there is a pipeline to god

At least
that's what they think
that's why
they keep chasing it
down every city street
every dark alley
every whorehouse
and dime bag
again and again

I don't know if it's addiction
or malnutrition
or capitalism
or a poor upbringing
by fucked up parents
in a fucked up society

But I do know
they are on a pipeline
to god

I don't judge them
on that

I'm on my own
pipeline to god

The skeetch Indian:

On public transit heading
downtown
I meet an Indian dude
who tells me he's heading
to the oil rigs soon
he just passed the
physical and drug tests
even though he ripped a couple
big fat rails days before the tests
he told me about smoking crack
how it never got it's claws
into him
as the bus weaved through town

Me and the Skeetch NDN
we talked about work
how much
we both hated this town
no money or opportunities here
a place where people came to die
then he was gone
off the bus
I was staring out the window
grey skies

Sault Ste. Marie:

Hung over bleary-eyed
I sit in a shopping centre
sipping the strongest coffee
I can find
this young kid
comes and sits at the table
next to mine
He tells me he's feeling lonely
he's homeless
his girlfriend
just kicked him out
She had another boyfriend
beat him with a baseball bat
He shows me the massive goose egg
on his head
red and painful
He eats pizza
we chat about his home
his reserve and his grandma
He tells me she is still walking around
on her own, even at 93 years of age
that she lost her hearing
when she was in residential school
because she was punished once by
being dragged by her ears

He showed me the fifty bucks
he made panhandling
told me he needed thirty more bucks
to get a bus home
I wanted to give him the money
I really wanted to
but I didn't know for certain
if he'd use it to travel home
or if he was a crack-head
I listened while he talked
after about 20 minutes
I couldn't take any more pain
or misfortune
I excused myself and left
As I headed out the door
he asked if I was going to finish
my food
I said "No, go ahead"

The Demon:

On the other side
of the country
reading some writing
I had done when I was 32
10 years past
what a strange decade

Three months on the road
it is easy to lose focus
to lose sight of the big picture
the goals
the dreams
the nightmares

There is a price
to pay
I've lost
as much as I've gained
I'm making peace
with that

I know I have to
spend even more time on the road
there's no end in sight

If you see me in a pub
come have a pint
with me
tell me all your sadness
let it all out

We'll have a good time
I promise

Alone:

Alone in a hotel
in a resort town
Alone in an airport bar
having a gin and tonic
Alone at 38000 feet
staring out the window
Alone on the road
driving through the mountains
thinking about the last ex
Alone in another hotel room
by the ocean during the winter
watching the reddest
sunrise I've ever seen
Alone getting drunk
in another strange pub
listening to locals
feel resigned to a life
of dread, monotony torture
it always amazes me
how easily they surrender
Alone at night
thinking of the relationships
I've pissed away
tonight it matters
I'd give anything
for a woman to walk
across the room
touch me again

Poetry Night:

It was an open mic night
downtown
I had been off the road
six months too long
I felt I was getting
A: bored B: stagnant C: rusty
I got off my ass
put my beer can down
headed for the gig

Upon arriving
surveying the obnoxious
yapping crowd
I felt instantly long in the tooth
we all put our names down
on a piece of paper
which went into a magic hat
where our names were drawn
the sequence of readers
for the night

It was actually great fun
hearing people read for the love of it
(not the carfac/author fees!)
the devotion
the dreams
the chance to be heard
by a room full of strangers
perhaps a bit of applause
a high five
a vindication that what you
are doing matters to someone
besides yourself

I'd been doing this
for nearly two decades
nothing surprised me
there was the bad poetry
the rhyming ones
the diva
the conspiracy theorist
the sensitive jock
the hipster

It was painful
the hipster read an awful
coming of age poem
I'm certain it meant a lot
drowned out by bad loops and beats
farting out of a little laptop
(I later realized this was this poet's ONLY poem
after attending several readings!)

We all clapped hands
some cheered
many were regulars
When it was my turn
I did nothing to call
attention to my experience
my books, art or films or music
I got up
read like everyone else
from crumpled sheets of paper
For the first time in years
I was a bit nervous
I felt a bit green
it went fine
after nearly 20 years
of this
working a room is easy
it's natural now
I love the roar of a roomful
of laughter as well as applause
sometimes I can even
get people doing "the wave"
if it's a big enough crowd

I read and it felt great
I've been going back
ever since
my own form of rehab
in a world I can't quit
We all backslap each other
into oblivion
again and again
until the next night:

Cabbies:

In Montreal I ask
for the hot spot
in town
we head to
St. Denis
eventually I end
up back at Fou Foune
Electrique
In Toronto I ask
for some weed
we head down
Spadina
I end up
at the Silver Dollar
then the Horseshoe Tavern
the bovine sex club
In Winnipeg
at the Windsor Hotel
watching Billy Joe Green
rip through a set so fucking loud
it melts my face off
I move outside
for some air and breathe
a little while having a smoke
watch some NDN kids beating
the shit out of each other
in a way more violent
more brutal than I would expect

I just stand there
another drag on my prayer stick
watching them knock teeth out
breaking ribs fingers jawbones hope
Everywhere I go
I talk to the cabbies
they know
the heartbeat
the pulse of the city
the inner workings
the places to avoid
the people to avoid
the clubs to avoid
then again
those same clubs
when you want to get
down and dirty

Always tip a cabbie well
I say
on the way to hell
you wanna be treated
just right

A hotel in another town:

I've finally reached the stage of better hotels
better food better booze
the hangovers are still the same
The sound of the traffic groaning
in the background
the vacuum cleaner bumping against
the wall outside my room as
the housekeeper noisily cleans
I just want to sleep this one off
that's all I want
but I can't
the young woman
is already up
wrapped in the hotel sheet
heading towards the patio

She opens the sliding glass door
I roll over and she points to the camera
tells me I should come
take some photos
of her outside
I grudgingly get up
we walk naked onto
the patio together
I start snapping photographs
of her
naked and glorious
On a cool winter morning
in a strange city
full of strangers
oddly no one looks up at us
as I furiously
snap photos

We both go back into
the hotel room
I have a shower
hoping to wash away
bad memories
maybe
just maybe
some of the stupid
things I've done

The stars:

Waiting in line
to board a jet
to roar down a runway
into a beautiful blue sky
full of happy people
lonely people
stars
of the literary
filmmaking
and creative arts

I meet them
at functions
note how many
are in excellent physical
condition, don't smoke or drink, well, maybe
red wine
they love antique shopping
in the different cities
we all visit

While they
enjoy fine dining
at exquisite breakfast restaurants
expensive upscale places
favourite nooks

I wander down
darker roads
absorbing the cities
of the night
stench of the rotting garbage
endless gritty pawnshops
yellow nicotine saturated air
cheap beer and loud pounding music
in a variety of pubs
Meeting up with the crazy, love-starved
hungry, manic energy
of the city

When we bump into
one another at various airports
I watch them make a scene when the plane
is delayed
shouting angrily at the flight staff
texting furiously on their phones
it is the end of the world
I count my blessings
feel genuinely fortunate
to even be here in the first place

Outside the window:

You stare outside the window
the spider slides down
a silk web in front of you
you don't notice
your eyes
dead
skin grey
all the blood in your body
sunk to your ass and feet
you are stiff
rigor mortis
you will remain this way
until the police
and paramedics break down
your door
your neighbours
finally complained about the smell
like blue cheese
like sweat socks
seeping from your apartment
Until then
you'll be sitting there
remembering your last good times
on this blue marble
hoping no one finds you like this

At 2:43 a.m.

I'm caught
 seized
by panic
 beast trapped in a net

As sun rises
over forest
fog rising
 mist settling
over long green
blades
of grass
gathering in buds
of flowers
waiting to bloom at dawn
I am a coyote
in the mountains
waiting to howl to hunt to kill

I hear a train in the distance
pounding against the rails
I remember
I am a man not a beast
I have court in the morning
a lawyer to meet
a statement to write
a soul to defend

When I realize
I have another
twenty-four hours
to redeem myself
to save myself
from the drama
of bad decisions

Watching you

as you watch
television
fills me with joy

I could stare into your eyes
for eternity
when I am not with you
I am filled with dread
a sad longing

one part me
one part your mother
you have the world
before you

don't think
that there are not times
when I feel regret
at the loss
of family life
for you
this was inevitable

but you carry the knowledge
of those before you
I know that you will not make the same
mistakes
errors in judgement
tact
whatever

despite the loss
I only wish
to provide you with what
I never had
a father

I will not
let time come to pass between us
as it has with my own father

Wake up:

You wake up
on her bed
it's nice and warm
traffic drones outside
she lays beside you
her long dark hair
always looks perfect
You trace the outlines of her face
with your finger and
move in for a kiss
as she continues to sleep
Watch her for a few moments
before slipping out of bed
down the hall to the bathroom
into the kitchen to make some coffee

As you wait for the water to boil
you wonder where she has been
all this time
while you were in the madhouses
the factories
the dead end jobs
the lovers each seeming
to be more crazy
than the other
All those horrible nights
those lonely nights
the ones you got down
prayed
for mercy
for tenderness
for a lover

those aching minutes
between drinks
in run down bars in other cities
some days raining
the window beating a pitter patter
of sorrow as the water
streamed down
some days sunny
but you still in the pubs
escaping the heat the sweat
the dust on your brow
sweat streaming down your back
sipping shitty beer
praying you don't end up like the rest

Where was she all that time
between the dark and night
it was in her eyes
you saw hope and promise
brilliant as a star cutting
through the darkness
saving you at last

The shh-ya-a and I

Broken Ribs:

A car crash:
concussion
broken ribs

I remember what she said
before she turned the car
hard on the corner and stepped
on the gas
making sure we'd flip
"you need me"
followed by
"you still love me!!!"

I clicked my seatbelt
just in time
we hit the ditch
the car groaned
flipped sideways
over and over again
the car
ended up back
on its wheels

our heads banged together
during the various vehicular
rotations through the air
but it still hadn't knocked sense
into either of us

I came to quickly
saw the dust
the smoke
felt goddamn lucky
she was still unconscious

I got out of the car
watched the city shimmer
checked for gas leaking
and explosive hazards

I woke her up

We were both able to walk away
after stuffing my socks
into the gas tank
and lighting them

Hey
we needed to see where we were going right?

As we limped down the road
the car exploded behind us
I hated myself
but at least we were still in love

I lied:

In another town far away
from her
we talk on the phone
we are both hung-over

I don't know about her room
but mine is spinning
it's a nice room
in a hotel

I fight back the urge to vomit
I lie to her
tell her I don't want a relationship
she says the same

I don't know if she is lying
I know I am

I watch crows flying outside my window
people jogging in the park across the street
the television jabbers on

I visualize pain
stabbing into my gut
a knifea bullet
as the words fly
from my mouth

The shh-ya-a and I

sat laughing
drinking
on the roof top
of the Balmoral

watched
the city eat
the people
humanity
fist itself
until

the night
came
stole
us
from
the roof
from our lives

The sik-la and I
sat up
late one
night
drank
      laughed
smoked
        swapped stories

of how we stole the sun
from people
      and their lives

he blanketed me
with his smooth
black feathers
told me secrets
of blood

The spa-achuh and I
told stories
of strength
and bravado

we talked
a tough tale
showed each
other scabs
scars
fresh gunshot
blasts

The sin-kyup and I
tricked people
from their
food
and clothing

he told me jokes
made me
laugh until I cried

The ish-shwelthtuh brought
me down
with his sad tale
of treachery

envy and lies
now I know
why he cries

The ska-lu-la
was so
serious
I couldn't crack a smile
from that hard bastard's face
who is next

The hal-lowt brought
me from
beginning
to the end

showed what really
was inside

we vowed to keep
that secret

Luck

sometimes
I have it

I say this and chant it
as I cross
a train bridge
that will lead me
to the
reserve

Luck
I chanted
as I carefully
placed each foot
on the broad beams
that carried
the trains
across the river

Luck
I prayed
I would not
fall into the freezing
water
or depression
or alcoholism
or fights
or
crime all over again

Luck
I chanted
desperately
as I ran down
a country road
by the city
reservation dogs
chasing me
biting at my heels

Luck
as I finally
reached the gas station
alive
bought my
tobacco without even
having to show them
my status
card

Luck
I walked
down the highway
towards the bridge
the city
home
the traffic lights
nearly blinding
me
I chanted
and chanted as I neared
the bridge
almost home
I kept thinking
almost home

Luck
As I passed
the last field
and started on the bridge
I saw
two horses
chasing each other
running
full throttle
free
to run into the night

Luck

Post-Colonial Setting

There's this one about the priest
and the indian:

" I am the way," says the priest
"You are what?" says the indian

" I am the way," says the priest
"The way of love and truth"

"You want to go hunting for moose?" replies the indian
"No, I am the way of clarity and understanding"

"You wanna swear at me and stare at my man-thing?"
"No my child, don't test my patience"

"Wild? Dressed? Paint chest? We go to war?"

silence then
blam

Thursday

"Hello Thursday
how you today?"

"FineI always am before
Friday."

"I know that
but what is new today?"

"I don't know
a man was found murdered
in a sweat-lodge
this morning."

"This morning? Hmmm.
That's no good, who was it?"

"I think it was DeeCee Scott."

"Hmmm what did he do
to deserve it? And in our mother's womb!"

"I don't know? Perhaps
he hurt someone."

"Yeah, but what about Billy Kinsella?
don't you remember?"

"OOOooh yeah! He was pulled in the thresher!"

"That was pretty gruesome!"

"Heh heh, yeah, maybe he thought it was magic, maybe he thought if he went in he'd be transformed into an
          indian?"

"Maybe DeeCee was just an asshole like Billy and he had it coming."

"Yeeeahhh, maybe."

"Uh! Grand Entry! We better get going!"

Scraps

Alone
decaying
we crawl
crawl through
the streets through
hands outstretched
through knees raw
bleeding
with feathers
bones
scalps
tufts of hair
all over our skin

we crawl
backwards
searching
for a voice
to all this madness
don't know where
to begin
a cancer of silence
has taken
over

now we can
only weave
stories
those who have the spare time
or spare change

I sift
through the scraps
of human remains
limp past
those already
drunk
already high
already dead
sleeping on the streets
desperate to forget
desperate to love

we fall to
crawling
through blackouts
the remains of those
we loved
we
go through bottles and darkness
laughing crying
bawling
through the streets
through dreams
we could never know or afford
crawling past clashing desires
of status
death

we crawl
we crawl
through the dark
through the dead
drowning in silence
worms in your
head
we scream you yell

this is a warning
we are coming

Confession

11: 01 pm
when the priest
told me
of
the innocence
he stole at the dog-gamned
residential school
I was neither amused nor surprised

as we walked
the cold
corridors
of the decaying school
he told me
told me of silence
the children
the darkness

he had no answer
when I asked him if he was
doing it for god
or because
he believed
the universal alibi

that natives were cold
uncouth
godless
heathen savages nobody

absolutely fucking nobody
in a new predominantly white-anglo country
would stand for them

no one
would give
two fucking shits about their screams
their torture
the abuse of them

11:23 pm
the priest had no answer when I asked
if he knew that south africa's apartheid system
    was based upon how kanada handled
        indigenous peoples?
no answers

but I knew he was holding out
on the answers
 just more
and more silence
welcomed me
" I see" I said to the darkness

 we walked
the halls we entered
a place
that had not yet been
repaired
" if this place could sing" he proudly proclaimed
" I can hear it"

the torturous wails a cacophony of sorrow
a hymn of flies
sickness death
 we walked through them
the voices
 cold chills
in a warm summer night

11:37 pm
I began
to feel an ache a heaviness
I thought of the books I had seen
page after page of
indian children
died of illnesses
mysterious
and otherwise

I thought of the crying children
who could not speak their language
could not see their parents
could not ask for medical treatment
could not hear the shaman singing
healing songs
they had nothing
nothing but pain

cramped in rooms of twenty
thirty and more children
boys segregated from girls
brother torn from sister
from mother
from father
grandmother and grandfather

no language
no ceremonies
nothing but fever
pain
piss and sores

11: 46 pm
holding his silence
like fine china
the priest
stood on end
prayed
not to god
but to the devil
to have mercy
on his soul

we carefully
climbed the stairs
that led to his private quarters
overlooked the fields
the playground below
he unlocked the door
at the top of the stairs
a single light bulb shone in the darkness
of the stairwell

yellow walls and stale smell of old papers and
books
we walked into his room
he gave me the key

11: 58 pm
nothing but the smell
of filth
 decay stood guard
over the mess of books boxes
scattered all over the floor
mouse shit everywhere nothing alive

12:01 am
he turned to me with a gleam
he began to laugh
a cold
hard shrill

all the while holding out his arms
for an embrace
"come,
  come to me,
    my child"

I ran
ran towards the door
ran from his cackling laugh
that crackled
into a shriek
high
wavering

I reached the door
a glimpse
of him
all dark
scary
with voices
running through him
running through him

I slammed the door
seized the key
rammed it
into the lock
 broke the key off

damning him
forever
in that room where so much
was lost

I will never forget
what he told me
what I saw

 long
after they tear
that damned building down

long after
 I turn to dust
he will still be there

with voices
going through him
going through him

Bakery, deli....

sitting on a bus
my eyes
pierce the eyes
of those fortunate enough
to drive automobiles
I see into their worlds
at fleeting instants
of invasion

beautiful woman
I see you stuck
in traffic
your child wailing
rolling away
in the seat behind you
come with me
my love
we will abandon
our worlds
pressures responsibilities
we will accommodate each other
submitting to our
desires fantasies needs
live
by robbing
convenience stores
declare war upon
the palaces of poverty
bingo halls
will no longer hold the poor
ransom

as we burn and pillage
our way across
Canada
the U.S.
ultimately the world
standing before you
I will take your purple
tank-top off
 taste you
tracing the lines
 curves of your body

It was stone

he was tired of stale
stone bread
he wanted something
sweet

like chocolate
like soda
sexoralsexheavysexcleansexwetsex
that's all we're really here for
the rest is all details he said

he dropped mushrooms
stood by the door
waiting for ecstasy
for god

I sat
in front of a computer
searching the net
for a good dominatrixxx
instead I found death
but
I kept searching

searching
to find the perfect
search engine

to find the perfect
curseword
to express how I felt
nothingwatching
maggots turn to flies

he waited for glory
I told him she wasn't coming
while I was
in front of the computer

plants
kept growing
dandelions
cypress
tumbleweed
blossoming
into the night

while we sat in his cocoon
waiting

waiting to be shit out like locusts
to begin again

Noshi

noshi
noshit
is am
ambivalent
arre ambiguous thought s   that strike
when you are hg high
impotent thogthss thogut thoughts

Noshi strikes again
thoughts of finding the cure
the cures
the identities
the gene that hidess
that kills
as you stumble down streets
in an old run down part of town
or run down an old part of town
that is now chic
remember
the

those poor motherfuckers who made the
sidewalks you stumble upon
the nignety year old sidewalks
that show the swings of the men's arms
who made them
swings that still swing
ninety year s   later

remember that

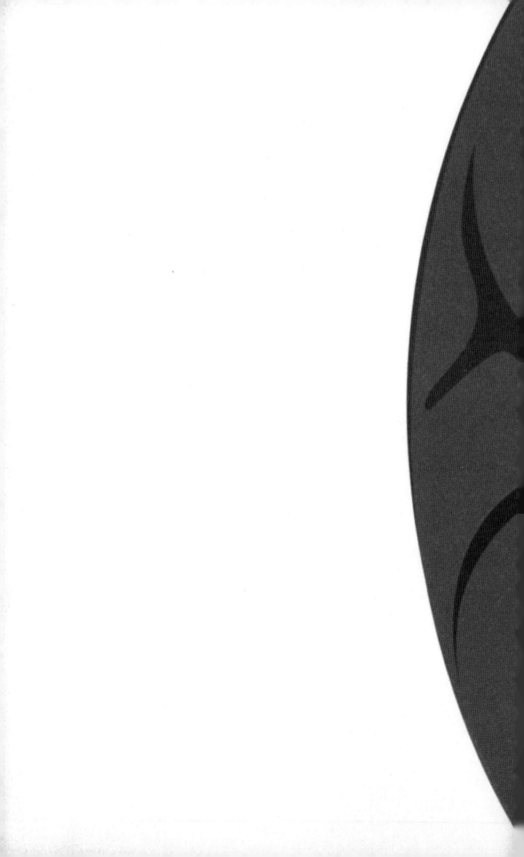

The flood and the fire
are true

Snow & Slush

are coming
you can feel it
the air bites when you
walk out the door
growling menacing
with a clean chill
that cuts your face
razorburn

the long nights are coming
the paranoia
thinking the sun has
a vendetta against you
it begins to slowly sink
after barely rising above the horizon

through the grey sky
the sky endlessly dead
all the time all the time all the time all the time
neither raining nor snowing
just grey   grey   grey   grey

the land sleeps
the green shrunk back defeated by ice and cold
hiding in the earth
deep in the trees

the earth turned against us in a gentle slumber
hoping we'll all be gone come springtime
cities dead and grey
all of us dead

in our cars/ homes/ boxes/ rectangles/ at the mall
that is what nature wants
all of us dead

that's why snow
and slush are coming

one day
we will all
wake up
stillborn

the only sound
that will be heard
will be
sparrows

cutting through the air
swarming
into the sky

More than a monster

you
poor
dirty
child

come in
sit awhile
you look tired
stressed

come in here
have some coffee
or milk
sweets
would you prefer?

I have not seen you
in such a while
You've changed so much
Has God found you?

Did you know
that you
have become
more than a boy
and more than a monster?

you have grown
now you turn
into a man

what did I tell you?

didn't I teach you anything?

Sarcos

everything seems too fast
the gigantic machines that were supposed
to free us
now dictate a more precise
doom

dreaming of spiders
gigantic caterpillars
about people I know
dead
haunting me

even about the
seventies
when I was only a kid
I thought the blonde from
abba was the shit
when I was young
living in surrey
delta
somewhere down there

I was afraid of girls
but pulled to some
one from Colombia—

now I'm feeling old
and stupid
now I have a daughter

I read that spanking is wrong
so I don't
they say it's bad for their cognitive development
the best thing to do is grab the kid and move
to a quiet zone
so much more different than when I was

the child of an alcoholic
single first nations mother
who went through the residential school system
then had me just when she was sixteen
my father twenty (also first nations)
that makes me first nations (I just thought I'd state the obvious
like so many others do)

we must have moved about sixty times
when I was growing up

I remember living in hotels
places like sparwood
castlegar flinflon
calgary
prince rupert

anywhere
so much different
than now
now that I am in charge of my own life
I believe insanity should be an inner thing
not something you subject others to

the other night
I was at a housewarming party
we were all drinking
roasting meat over an open flame
other pagan rituals

a friend of mine commented
 how canadian my kid is
"she's the daughter of an aboriginal
  and an immigrant, I mean how much more
   canadian can she get?
    that's how this country
      was built..."

cleverly
I said, "fuck you,"
 we all had a good laugh

I got up
 walked over to the balcony

overlooked
the north and south thompson
rivers converging
silently during twilight
two dark snakes wriggling down the valley
to bond
in the darkness

I saw venus twinkling in the dark blue sky
green
red
I heard someone flipping the meat
the sizzle of new fat burning on the fire
down the valley the western sky was turning pink
then orange
overhead it was blue getting dark
more stars came out
with no moon the night was theirs ours

as the city lights over kamloops
came flickering on
one by one
I prayed for the aurora borealis

prayed that this time—
with good drinks
friends fiends
roasting meat—would never end

wantinggiant praying mantises
to clamber over the roof
grab us one by one

cracking our heads open
in their giant mandibles

Rattle:

Four or five rattles
arranged on a brightly colored
star blanket
on the altar

looked like buckskin
so smoothly wrapped around
a gourd

a couple had horns
like a devil

others
had horsehair
streaming down
from the handle

they looked pretty important
I'd seen them lots over the years

all over the place
in old
nearly abandoned
rez churches
people's houses
treatment centers
sundances
vision quests

all of the rattles
in a row

My uncle
Matoa Omani
growled at everyone
telling them stories
about his journey
how it brought him
to the Red Road
from the darkness
almost boasting about it

my other Mach-Peya Tekula
sat silently broodingly
playing with his braids
his moustache
patiently waiting
for the ceremony to begin
to make
stars of them both

then it was over
the speeches
the warnings
the heeding for anyone
without the will
or nerves
to leave

the darkness
fell upon us all
a darkness like no other

As the ceremony started
I thought back
to my first sundance
under the endless blue
skies of wolf point
that first night
at my uncle's house
staring up at the vast
night sky
lying on a bedroll
more stars than I'd ever seen
glimmering silently
the universe holds so many
secrets

As I lay there I knew
my blood would be spilt
beneath the blue sky
a lot of blood would
be spilt

I watched
as the sparks dropped down
a sign that the grandfathers
and grandmothers
were arriving

in a few moments
the rattles would be flying around
the room in total darkness

A room full of people
full of people
on the floor
huddled together
a darkness so complete
not even a sliver of light
could pierce through

the whole
building would begin shaking
the floor rumbling
vast herds of buffalo
deer
elk
circling outside

sometimes you could hear
bears growling fiercely
standing and scraping
at windows and doors

then the flap of wings
everywhere
huge wings
cooled you off every time
they passed over you

I fought hard the urge
to reach out
to try to grab a rattle
as it flew overhead

shaking like rattlesnake tails
everywhere at once

Flashes between the fire:

Staring at the darkness
between the flashes
of the fire
faces
and places
forests
and fields
highways
and cities
rattle through my head
a train
at dawn
after a night of tall tales
and fine whiskey

I write this
as a warning
a scream
on the edge of the mountain
do not follow
in my footsteps
choose another profession
see another light

untangling myself
from umbilical tombs
barren cities
scraped of all that is left

The ones I love:

The birds
The leaves
My children

You want to fight me?

I can become on fire in an instant

Racing without abandon
160 miles per hour
With a pack of lies
and a wall of dirt
against an ocean of expectation

I'm ready

To crack my skull
 my ribs
against a night sky
 a million stars
falling

The water leaks:

The water leaks
from a broken faucet
the grime
mildew along the corners
of the wall and the edge
of the tub

Outside it rains and rains
wearing us all thin
to rag water
in a bucket of oil

The traffic drones
children scream outside
playing in the rain
jumping in the puddles

I'm in a strange town
on the edge of the ocean
with a beautiful native woman
I could fall in love with
I fight it everyday
like a heavyweight match

The city is drowning
my eyes are burning
with her temptation

I lay in bed listening to the rain
the children
My own children
far away in the mountains
in a dry
dust blown town

I haven't forgotten them
I haven't left them
I am just waiting
until the fires subside
between their mother and i
my heart
fragile as an eggshell

My two-year old daughter's smile
My son's laughter
Our blue-eyed baby's endless chewing on her
finger

The hot-springs:

We drove down somewhat
spontaneously irresponsibly perhaps idiotically

I needed to see something different
to get out of town
to forget a few things
we loaded up the car
with the spirit of adventure
hit the road
hit it hard
driving all afternoon towards
The Kootenays

Finally
we can drive no further
the road gets steeper
the snow deeper
after several charges
up the hill and nothing
I know we are screwed
7 km still
to the hot-springs

With a 40 kg backpack
a baby
more gear still to pack
up goddamn hill after hill
another 7 goddamn
kilometers
I seriously question
my sanity
I begin the slog
in my skate shoes

Half a kilometer up the road
some dudes show up
on a ski-doo with a sled
offer us a ride
we gladly accept
throwing in heavy gear
jump in the back
heading off to the hot-springs

After seemingly
endless turns
and hills
we get there
hike down
a near-suicidal path
of logs, stumps, loose ground
getting to the hot-springs

which are full of drunken Albertans
blowing back some joints
Albertan whiskey
beers
god knows what else
while we unpack
get ready for the hot-springs
which I pray are as good
as I've been told

We find a hot-spring
not full of drunk obnoxious people
get in the achingly
warm water
begin relaxing
to the sounds
of hoots and hollers
it is what I imagine a wild westtown
sounds like

I realize
I should get a fire started
drag my ass out of the water
head up to the fire pit
it's so humid
the wood we brought
instantly damp

a survey of the campground
reveals that there's absolutely
nothing to burn
everything worth
burning has been burned

I stumble
through the dark
the bush
begin stripping and scratching cedar bark
boughs
in hopes of getting something
to get the fire going
any sort of fire

back to the fire pit
I see that everything
just gathered
is already wet
soaking fucking wet
curse myself
for not thinking clearly

the only things near dry
are two Leonard Cohen books
 I grudgingly pull
out of my backpack

I hear the Albertans
the horrible Yee-hawing
 screaming
 their dogs barking
 wait for the sound
of guns to go off
but they don't

page by page
I begin tearing up
the Leonard Cohen books

We make a ritual out of it
having a drink
reading a poem
crumpling it
into the fire
a laugh a smoke

To hell with it:
I think to myself
throw another poem
into the fire

The flood and the fire are true:

The bone and the gristle are true
The snake and the bite are true
The corpse and the stench are true
The homeless and the poverty are true
The knife and the meat are true
The flawed and forgotten are true
The lover and the baby are true
The street and exhaust are true
The smoke and the sewers are true
The sunset and the night are true
The moon and the lovers are true
The blood and the blade are true
The planes and the ground are true
The thunder and the lightning are true
The pawnshops and the hunger are true
The addictions and alcohol are true
The need and the bills are true
The struggle and the hope are true
The family and the love were true

I lost my way
and in turn
I lost them

now struggle through
to find my way back
to a beginning without them

Warfare

somewhere in monte-carlo carlo
there is a man smoking
a fine cigar

standing on a balcony overlooking
the mediterranean

maybe he can see the stars
maybe he can see the moon

sweat is beading on his brow
despite the cool sea breeze

the waves are making him thirsty
dreaming of singapore
skyscrapers

I think there is a curse fitting for him

wherever you are right now
carpe diem   live

While you slept
I ate the world

While you slept I ate the world:

The valley was covered in gold, everywhere gold, on the buildings, the streets, on the junkies and the needles they leave behind the ice rink. There was gold along the river where children swim and play. In the hills there was gold and in this room, alone with you, it was gold. In the mind was where a person's fortune lay, shimmering in the dark with sapphires, rubies, gems and gold, all the wealth in the world that one could think of, castles, kingdoms lay waiting for the taking. All you had to do was dream them, and make them real. Of course, that was too easy, and people instead chose to do it the hard way and work for the rest of their lives.

All the while the treasure of life passed them by, they kept their heads down and worked ever harder as they enviously spied those who took the easy way out and had found their windfall. I sit and watch my babe sleep, the sunrise and the valley slowly come to life and I wonder when we will find our treasure, or if we already have. No, I doubt it, because there is more to life than this narrow sliver of land, crowded with buildings, morons, and hunger. Every now and then you could see it, a glint of hope here and there, but it would disappear with the wind, only to return at night in our dreams.

A path here unfolds, we should follow it, but beware, because along the way are traps, seduction, and lies. Along the way are burdens for the unwary to pick up and carry if they are so inclined and foolish, but there are also pitfalls of temptation and fire as well. If one is careful and conscious then the path is easier, there is greater opportunity to find their riches, to live their lives satisfied and full. Instead of the empty, desperate, paranoid, and deluded ways that so many others scramble about and follow.

Walking along the river with Christina we find a dock and sit and watch the world pass us by. The healing power of water should not be under-rated, that flowing creek, the river, a lake. When I finally left my family, I would spend time with my daughter at the river, in fact an entire spring and summer at the beach, just walking along feeding the birds, throwing rocks at the vast abyss. She enjoyed herself, and I have many wonderful memories and photographs of this era of my life and hers, despite the ache and pain of having to leave her stranded with her mother.

I cast many a stone filled with hate, rage and frustration into the river, cursed the sky under my breath, and all the happy, successful boring people that walked along the beach up on the sidewalk. They seldom strayed from the path while I would do anything to burn it. I took my daughter's hand. I would bring her with me given the chance. The river was powerful and healing, it took my rage away, down to the lake, then further out, winding along towards the big blue Pacific Ocean.

Carrying my burden past villages, chapels, campfires and anglers, over ruins and bodies, through rapids and rafters, all the way down the Fraser Canyon and out far into the sea, then the ocean, away from me. My pain and agony, now joining the rest of the world's shit and slime, forever gone, freeing me to slip through night after night, through hills of sage, and forests of pine and fir, alive with the power of the night.

As Christina and I walked along the beach, the stench of the rotting salmon and drying seaweed overpowering and nauseating at once, I remembered what I had set free and wondered if the dead salmon had seen ghosts of my past along the sea floor. The sky began to get dark and grey, the wind picked up and we decided to make for land, away from the punishing stench and the ghosts of the sea.

My bad fortune was slipping away, joining the burdens that I had let go into the river just like these venomous serpents feigning friendship and brotherhood. I've stumbled and fallen, but never cut them up as I fell. Now as the day comes to an end for me in this town, I relax and know that they will still be here in ten years' time.

Nothing will have changed, except more lines in their fat, sagging faces. They'll be more desperate to cling to anything that shows promise, to drain all the hope away to feed their own withered sacks of spirit.

The only way out was to leave, and never come back, burning the trail behind as you leave, so none could follow and find you. I knew that many a time, people had planned my funeral, hatched a death for me, telling any excuse as to why I had left them to rot, when really their own actions brought it about. I had a list of those that I would slip back and steal in the night, because you couldn't build an army alone, and you couldn't fight the world by yourself, that would only lead to madness. Staring out the window, I knew in a few hours the stars would be shining down, and perhaps the sky would be clear for us to see. Tonight I would sleep, and in my dreams find my way out of here, slowly bringing back the plans so I could finally escape, before the darkness and damage of this town destroyed my dreams.

Poverty strikes you again
and again like a cobra.

I'm still awake, which is pretty amazing, but I'll be sleeping soon.It's these long days that are sure get to you when you're not ready. I'm not sure what's worse, working all the time or not working all the time and expecting money to fall out of the sky into your waiting hands. Poverty is a rich man driving you mad by whispering into your ears all the secrets of life, and poverty is what wakes you in the middle of the night,when you realize you are starving but have no food. All of the nightmares pounding in your head to the steady rhythm of your heartbeat, that is what poverty is, rolling out the monsters, the ghosts and all your dark nights one by one forever.

Poverty is a needle in the gutter and you collecting cans, counting pennies and thinking about all the money you've ever wasted on cigarettes, drugs, alcohol, and stupid purchases. I know poverty is losing all those years in bars, strip clubs and in houses high on drugs or the time lost waiting to score drugs. Poverty is still the rich man in your head, screaming at you about what a failure you are and to get up and out of bed and to get a job. Poverty is waking up after a particularly bad night and wondering where all that time goes in the midst of a black out.

When you look in the mirror and are not certain of who is staring at you, let me tell you, you can rest assured it is poverty. In a world of excess knowing a few truths makes all the difference, but not being able to do anything about it but swim with the current and let the sour taste of lies burn like gasoline, that is poverty. Watching your parents beat one another is another form of poverty, and wondering what life is all about as it burns away all around you is even more poverty. Lost at the racetrack after betting your last dollar and losing, then coming home hungry and nothing to take away the pain, that is poverty.

Alone in the city and pills for breakfast is nothing poverty. Feeling nothing towards death, that is poverty, and the absence time is further evidence of poverty. When you burn like fire and are violent and/or emotional when under the influence, someone better tell you what poverty is all about. Again, poverty is the rich man who runs the world by a machine, holds every dream in a vault, counting each second as a heartbeat and each minute as a lifetime, gone, sold, bartered away by the hour until the end of time. But that is life kid, and you better get fucken used to it, you hear me?

Teeth in the grass and bones in the leaves.

I'm so tired of reading. No, that is not true, but I am tired of being hit over the head by time and waiting for grants and things to happen. I'm tired of confusion and exhausted by the skeletons of the past that rise each night from the grave of memory. Constantly they scrape on the windows and some turn to dust and slip through cracks in the window and under the front door to sneak into our home and into our minds. Filling the nights of rest with hours of trauma and relived memories and monsters and demons toiling at the art of torture. They rise to life in the flame of an argument and you don't notice until you are hot and flush with anger and suddenly realize the words coming out of your mouth are exactly like what your mother or father would say.

Then shame begins to burn bright, a cold shimmering flame, bright as the sun and blinding as you struggle to bottle back the pressure chamber of your mind. Stress and anger from years before suddenly blast forward with little provocation and you realize that you are full of pain and somehow have to begin the long, difficult task of siphoning off the poisonous bile from your soul. You must do this before it gets stained black forever dooming you to return to this hell again and again. I wake up and find myself along a barren stretch of road, walking towards the sunrise on the shoulder of the crumbling black and grey asphalt.

The sky is dark and cloudy while there seems to be nothing and no one for as far as I can see in this prairie flatland. Is this how life is supposed to be? Where am I going and what will I do when I get there? I want to walk into the middle of a field and dig towards salvation. I think about the past and how it worms into the present, tunneling through time to rear up and crawl up your back, getting you when you least expect it. These are the gifts of dysfunctional parents who had no parents and no language, only priests and nuns in a residential school while their parents anxiously waited for the return of their stolen children.

Some probably waited sober and worked the land if they had such a luxury, while others forced off the land into reserves probably lost all hope and clutched at the bottle like a hangman holds the noose. People always ask me why Indians are so screwed up and this is but one reason why we are the way we are and no, I have no idea how it will end. Somehow, we are the children who must begin putting it back together, what we don't finish our children will. Our children will learn what to do with the pieces of our people.

This work that we do will take generations until we arewhole again, no longer walking the cities and small towns in a stupor of alcohol, drugs, confusion, pain and hate. There will be teeth in the grass and blood on the ground until it all comes together. Outside the sky is getting brighter and the day is upon us all now. I know some of us will get up running and some will crawl, while others will shuffle through their day in a confused swamp and nothing will happen and they will get nowhere. This is how it is and you can't save anyone but yourself, someone once told me.

Now I sit and write and write and write, try to use words to find my way from the labyrinth and the clutches of the monster that is eating everyone else and my dreams. Outside the wind blows and the people I have seen today, all the insanity and bloody greed, only make me loathe it all a little bit more.

The words will pour out of my head, clear and angry, calm and bitter, hostile and intense because that is all I've known. I think about my role models parental and otherwise and know that I'm fucked, but so is everyone else, and that is why humanity is flawed. We are not diamonds, we are coal, we need pressure to change. I know it as do you, so what next will you do to save the world or yourself?

In the meantime, I will sit in this small room with a nice view of the park and rot in a small town, and sweat it all out: the storms, the drunks, the cravings, the hunger, the rage, the depression and the mood swings until I get it together. Some have waited their entire life for enlightenment and I'm prepared to go the distance because there is simply nothing else for me to do.

I know that life isn't for those born with a head start or a curse or a burden, it is for everyone. We must figure it out before every grain of time has slipped through our hands. Somewhere is a cave with an old piece of parchment that has the answers we are looking for, but as long as we continue to march to the sound of money it will never be found. My lungs ache for fresh air and my nerves wait to be healed. I bide my time knowing that sooner or later, we'll get it together.

Arbour

I wake up and stare at the ceiling, and for a second, remember
a time when I woke up in a teepee and stared through the
smoke hole at the top and saw blue sky. I remember crawling
out of that teepee and looking around the arbour. It felt as
though I had woken up after falling into a time-trap, somehow
waking in another century. A morning fog was clinging to
the dozen or so other teepees, everyone was clambering out,
dressed in traditional regalia and ceremonial clothes. It was so
surreal, white fog twisting through the tiny village of teepees,
and at the same time, it was beautiful and tragic.

I knew it was only a brief feeling of peace, of belonging, of
being in a village of family, not in a city full of strangers. All
too quickly that feeling faded and the Sundance was over, I
was back on the long road back into the modern world and all
that came with it. I can clearly remember sitting and staring at
the South Hills of Dakota, the sad feeling of having to let that
vibe go, of the community I had left in the hills behind me.
The long winding road opening before me.

Today, when I woke up, I wanted that feeling back, of not
being alienated in a city. I wanted to wake up and see the
pale blue sky of the dawn and know that everything was
going to be alright. That strangers, monsters or wolves didn't
surround me and there would be a warm fire, and good food
and friendly, talkative company full of jokes and great stories.
Not this, this cold city staring back at me all angry, jagged and
dark, the lights gleaming down like feral eyes in the darkness
and barren parks, empty parking lots and icy long boulevards.

This place of forgotten faces and names, passing by like
shadows. Reflections in windows of storefronts only show
strangers and no one knows the next one beside them. We
long for company in a sea of unfamiliar faces and gather in
places of business just to feel close to another being. Even if
it is only for a couple of minutes, it is so much better than the
lonely place called home.

A box in a vast mausoleum where we sleep a few hours and get ready to face another long day of arduous tasks and tests that will never be completed or done away with, because we know they will be waiting again the next morning. Life is one long ache of loss, of alienation, of wanting and needing to belong to a larger whole, but we have lost the myth, the connections that bind us.

Each day, when we wake up, we don't know what we want or what we long for, only wish that aching feeling to subside and the anxiety that plagues millions to go away. I wake up and stare at the city and wonder why we have lost our way, and when did it all begin to slip away from our grasp. Who or what was at the root of our undoing, was it lust, greed or something else getting in the way of the larger dream of our culture and society?

I stare out the window and watch the morning traffic begin to trickle into the city and know that another day in the machine is about to begin. Down the hall my family sleeps. I wonder what we are going to do in the future, will we live here, or will we have to move away? Continually searching for something to fill the void and to release us from this poverty, this struggle and mess of desperation.

I hate this world and yet pity it, because it is such a mess. So many mangled people I meet along the way, purely oblivious to the miracle around them. Just wandering day to day like an idiot, pissing away life and wondering what next to do and what next to buy. As if that was what life was all about. I prepare for another day of battle in the trenches. I know that one day soon, the generals will have their heads on pikes.

A view from the 63rd floor.

I wake with a start, ripped from a bizarre sequence of dreams that bring the dead to life and resurrect old friendships. In disbelief I check to make certain of my surroundings, then begin to stretch out the night of sleep and quietly slip out of bed. After doing the usual morning rituals, washing up, preparing coffee, I sit and stare out the window at the gloomy, grey weather of the Fall. Outside, the roads are slick and the trees are still, while the sky above is a solid wall with no blue or breaks in the clouds, I can hear it drizzling on the pavement. I think about the people I saw in my dreams. I wonder if some dreams are premonitions and things will happen accordingly after the dream, as in, you will meet the people you haven't seen for ages.

I start to imagine living on the 63rd floor of a building overlooking Central Park. I get the idea from looking at a recent copy of Architectural Digest. This is a magazine I pick and read from time to time, and daydream that I'm filthy rich, a totally decadent Vesterner carrying the triumphant, blood soaked flag of the right wing and all that is Capitalism. Unconcerned with the exploitation, the losses, the bankruptcy, the insider trading, and the avarice as rapacious and repugnant as it can be, as the beast scours the earth of every last shred of worth. Imagine greed as a monster, one with a million heads and gargantuan in size, blocking out the sun and toppling buildings, crushing cities and leveling mountains.

Greed that is green, and yellow, and orange and blood red and blue when it wants to seep into people's minds to send them off shopping, hoping a trip to the mall will cure their blues. All the bright and dark colours of hate and love and death and fury and peace, wrapped in tattered chunks of fabric stapled to this monster as it glides effortlessly through the night, changing shape and appearance for anyone and everyone.

For some greed is a crack pipe and for others it is an empty needle and for some it is a car, for others it is money in the bank, and for a few others it is clothes. While for some it is a big house with a beautiful view, a million-dollar view and nothing in the soul, the bank or the mind except for the empty, clanging sounds of malice and envy. I see it everyday and it seeps into my heart and poisons my mind when people drive by. I loathe the system because I can't understand how some can have so much while others have so little.

Then I think of the beast and I think of the monsters running around in people's heads, barking at them, ordering them to get up and fight, to spend to get every last thing possible because if they don't then someone else will. That would be wrong and we are so alienated, we justify everything. There's an excuse bought and sold in the papers, in ideologies, in the media, always a way to make sense of the world if you really look for it.

The meaning is hidden, locked beneath an ocean of swirling snakes and long, dark grass while the ignorance shines brilliantly on a pedestal. I can hear it everyday when I wake up, that beautiful voice of greed echoing across the city like a church bell for Sunday Mass. A smooth voice beckoning us to get out of bed one more time and into the trenches for another eight hours for slaughter, for sacrifice and for money. I hear it now saying, "I am the way, follow me to fulfill your dreams," and I want to, and I try.

But it's all a lie, a clever one that seduces us all into sacrificing, family, friends, life and all in between. It's all just so we can toss a few more luxury items onto a big pile of crap in the basement, the closet or the garages that I walk past and see, spilling goods and memories of services across the driveway and into the streets. People don't care. I'm chastised for being poor by my own family and friends, for being a dreamer, for being driven by a slightly different ideology that makes me think before I purchase, before I spend another eight hours away from my family.

At least my girlfriend is not wanting me to head out of town like so many men I see and know, having to work on the oil rigs in Alberta, or the resource industries in Northern B.C. or even the Northwest Territories. Places that are being mined and forested and picked clean 24 hours a day of every last thing we deem necessary to increase our wealth while spiritually we die everyday. No one addresses this: as long as we believe we are never going to die, why bother right?

But that's the ironic part, we will all die, you, me, him, her, and everyone in between is going to die. We're going to rot or be burned to nothing one day. Everything we slaved a lifetime for will simply be given away or auctioned off. Any money in the bank will be spent and in a few years, it will all be a memory without a tear.

No one addresses the soul, the spirit or whatever you want to call it, because that is only something you do on death's doorstep. I've seen it happen many times, the realization of mortality and fatality closing in makes people beg, cry and plead for more time, for family they ignored for years while chasing the vault. I've seen rich people die alone, gasping and fighting for every last breath of life, and I've seen people surrounded by family and friends as they drift off into the abyss.

Both were scared of what next. I know this whole "God" thing works on a local level, but once you start traveling the world, then things change and you see that there is more to it than that. Perhaps we're older souls than we're told, or perhaps this is all just a place for us to come and learn about the physical, the material manifestations of everything beautiful and horrible about the soul.

Sometimes I wonder if we are universal beings of energy and light that never die, but only live and float through existence after existence, because energy cannot be destroyed, or so the physics books taught me. I mean think about it, if we were all horses, God would be a horse, because we give this world meaning in order to cultivate a sense of being.

Instead, we're humans and we are built in the likeness of God, so God looks like a human, how convenient. Anyway, what I'm trying to say is that as I sip my expensive coffee and think about all this shit, is that anything is possible. All you have to do is get out of bed to pursue it, and find out for yourself.

Stoned

In the mouths of so many are the same old stories, of making
it, of dreaming, of working, of dying and fucking and pain and
prison and wanting. It is all such bullshit. As Christina chops
broccoli, and carrots and sweet potatoes and yams and ginger
and garlic to prepare soup for our dinner tonight, our son
sleeps down the hall in our bed. He lays there, softly breathing,
cuddled up to a stuffed bear, sandwiched between two pillows
so he doesn't fall off the bed. Across the road the rich, old man
pulls up in his luxury vehicle, I finger him as he looks up.

I want him to know that one day we will come for him, his
food and his car and his house and everything that he has
that the rest of us do not. I want him to know he will pay
like we pay in blood and time everyday. I want him to know
the reason that the system will fall apart. It is because we are
tired and hungry and sick of being tied behind bars so the
men in dark uniforms that appear in our minds can beat the
system and the lies and the fear and the power of authority
into our hearts. I watch him pull his luxury vehicle into the
garage that is beneath his fortress of a house and know that
his time is soon.

The grey outside and all that comes with it is driving me
mental. I turn all the lights on in the house and curl up into
a ball and pray for it all to go away. Nothing happens. I am
given no divine sign, no burning objects like a t.v. or the stereo
blasting a message of faith to me. I get up and stare out the
window and write like mad so I don't go mad. I cried earlier
today while watching a program about the Kahnesatake
Mohawk, the hell they went through because some rich
assholes wanted to extend their golf course into the final shreds
of Kahnawake Aboriginal land, not far from the Kahnesatake.

The land was obviously a very old cemetery, yet that wasn't enough to stop the hungry developers. The Mohawk were not going to take it any longer. At one point during the tense standoff, under the threat of imminent attack from the Canadian military and thousand or so police officers sent in to assist the soldiers in pulverizing a couple hundred "renegade" Aboriginal warriors, the elderly and the woman and children were evacuated from the Reservation.

As the convoy of vehicles left, they had to cross a bridge that lead into Montreal, but of course, a lot of things happened along the way and they were stalled on the bridge for a couple hours. During this time, a few thousand angry white people had gathered on Montreal side and were waiting for the convoy with stones. When the convoy was finally allowed to leave the bridge and the Reservation, they were pelted with thousands and thousands of stones by a bloodthirsty mob of ignorant savages. They hit elderly men, women, babies, and children with their stones of hatred. I wonder who cast the first stone?

This is Canada and this is how Aboriginal people have been treated for centuries, always left outside to freeze and die, or to be punished, pushed off their land for never "developing" it into something worthwhile. Nothing is ever enough and nothing is ever right for the angry mob. I know that had we all perished in the first onslaught of settlers and explorers, they would have been all the happier.

But, we have not, and we will not disappear as has been claimed for centuries. I watched the stones pelt the cars and smash through windows denting hoods, fenders, roofs and trunks. I knew that we had a long way to go to any sort of equality or civility. I watched children cry when they were remembering the incidents. I cried a little. I knew there was nothing worse than the human being. Truly, the wrong species has inherited the planet.

Stream

on a perfect morning
I finally decide
to let out
a flood of thoughts
the constant rampage
through my head

I must bleed these
words from my
cranium out of my
ears onto the paper
into your eyes flowing
through your mind
leaving me alone
at last

leaving you peering
into the edge of darkness
an abyss of night
a hymn of flies
the roar of madness
the silence of melancholy
the hunger of addiction
leaving me at last

Kill to Survive

there is snow
in the mountains
snow in the mountains of kilimanjaro in
the seven sisters the rockies on those fasting
mountains that do not look like white elephants
but rather mountains
that look like sleeping bison
bears
and have trees that bare the last leaves of
fall
fall from
naked limbs
that stretch
stretch
for stars for sky
I beg
for mercy
beg for fucking mercy beg
in the cold
there is no mercy
the falling sun
a red sky
leaves
and dreams blow
across the town
the moon
rise
above frozen water
and
shards of glass
are you crazy
are you fucking crazy I scream
"I hear voices" you tell me
"I hear nothing" I tell you

I hear nothing calling me from
underground
and in caves hiding
you forget
you forget
what I am
to say to tell them
to the dead that walk through the bottles and cans
with your name stitched to their lips
they are all around
you
still you do nothing
nothing but follow
the leaves needles condoms
and garbage that
falls to the ground
still
you don't know
who you are
or where you are
what's going on
you are in another city
the cold hard street
stares up at you again
mocking your loneliness and pathetic
despair
rain comes
as you collapse
but still
you
know nothing
about who you are
where it hurts
at the end
of each day
armies clash in the night
as do you
with your
past

The pull over:

Out in the forest
in - 25 degree weather
my cousin and I trudge
through the bush picking up trees
branches
stumps witches hair
anything for a fire
my lungs ache in the cold
in that temperature
everything becomes painfully
labourious
It's nearly midnight
there's enough snow
on the ground for moonlight
to Guide our search
to scavenge enough wood
for a fire
to keep from freezing to death
At least the beer's cold
I think out loud and we both laugh
finally gathering enough
for a fire
a ritual
a rite of passage
a bullshit session in the forest
As we sit
by the fire
downing beers
We watch the moon rise
above the trees
jagged and dark against
a starless night

We let the fire die down
the dirty jokes
get quieter
we get back in the truck
drive 20 kilometers
back into town

It's nearly 3:30 am
I motion to the right
in a fork in the road
bad move
The cops are there
we get pulled over
fines and a suspension
from driving
I take off down the road
while my cousin gets
hauled off to jail
I get to a gas station
they won't let me inside
because of the rules
They're afraid of getting robbed
but I'm freezing cold
shiver and cough
outside for 30 minutes
until a cab arrives

I tell him to take me to the hospital
where I'm told several hours later
that I have pneumonia
I need to go home
rest
I have no money
so how do I rest?
I go home
3 days later
I get a notice in the mail
I've been awarded a grant
to write this poem
to tell you

Sometimes things work out
sometimes they don't

Bathe

draw a bath
   cup your hands
 hold the water
hold your breath

outside
the clouds
   say that it should be raining
but it isn't

in the forest
    there is rain
 streaming
   down leaves
dripping off branches
pooling on the ground

cool rain
in the mountains
coming down
like pins
  and needles

  on your face
     your arms
       your hands
   scream for more

you could be reborn
you could be forgiven
you can't

you drink the rain

Glossary

hal-lowt ~ Eagle (N'lakapamux)
ish-shwelthtuh ~ Loon (N'lakapamux)
sarcos ~ flesh (Latin)
shh-ya-a ~ Crow (N'lakapamux)
sik-la ~ Raven (N'lakapamux)
sin-kyup ~ Coyote (Secwpemc/N'lakapamux)
ska-lu-la ~ Owl (N'lakapamux)
spa-achuh ~ Black Bear (N'lakapamux)

About the Author

Chris Bose is a writer, multi-disciplinary artist, musician, curator and filmmaker.

He is a founding member of the Arbour Collective, an Aboriginal arts collective based in Kamloops, with a national membership. He is also a workshop facilitator of community arts events, digital storytelling, art workshops with people of all ages and backgrounds, curatorial work for First Nations art shows and projects, research and writing for periodicals across Canada, project management and coordination, music festival producer, mixed-media productions, film, audio and video recording and editing, and more.

He is of the N'laka'pamux/Secwepemc Nation in BC, and currently spends his time in Kamloops BC. His previous books include *Stone the Crow* (Kegedonce Press, 2009), and *The Apology* (Unit/Pitt 2013)

His favourite drink is a double greyhound. His life is a secret. The closer you are means the further you have to go.

You can download some of his music for free here: soundcloud.com/chris-bose

Visit his blog, *urban coyote teevee*: findingshelter.blogspot.ca

Acknowledgements:

This book and almost everything I do creatively couldn't be done without the support, understanding, love and backing of many people and organizations. The Bose kids, their mothers, my mum (for tolerating my dreams all these years), my many aunts and uncles, my many brothers and sisters, Johnny, Tugboat, Sandra, Lori, Rainbow (Rambo) and Lorne plus the one and only Timothy G! as well as the crew and family that is the Arbour Collective, Shealagh deDelley, Nigel Szigeti, Byron Steele, Bracken Hanuse Corlett, Dean Hunt, Sharon Shuter, Cease Wyss, Garry Gottfriedson, Richard Van Camp, Tania Willard, Nacoma George, Paul Donald, January Rogers, Ellijah Jules, Shawna Seymour and B.O.A., Elwood Jimmy, Grant Hartley, Caroline Dick, Starleigh Grass, Warren Dean Fulton, Lanny MacDonald, Battery Opera and David Mackintosh, the Unit/Pitt Gallery and Keith Higgins and crew, Kegedonce Publishing and Kateri Akiwenzie-Damm, Renee Abram and Joanne Arnott for editing my books, the Enowkin Centre, Tracey Kim Bonneau, Jeanette Armstrong, the Ullus Collective, Victoria and Richard Armstrong, Mariel Belanger, the Cooksferry Indian Band and Dave Walkem, the N'laka pamux Nation, the Secwepemc Nation, the BC Arts Council and Walter Quan, the First Peoples' Cultural Council and Cathi Charles Wherry, Steven Davies, the Canada Council and Noel Habel, the Kamloops Art Gallery, Jann, Diane, Emily, the Alternator Centre for Contemporary Art, Arnica Artist Run Centre and Linda Jules, Kamloops Arts Council, CICAC (RIP) and Ashok Mathur, Jonathan Dewar, Bill Greene, 180 projects including Andrea, Devin, and Jason (OZO!), Thompson Rivers University, Algoma University, Shingwauk University, School District 73, Caroline Hilland, Colleen Minnabarriet, Brooke Haller, and the many teachers and administrators that have brought me throughout the province and across Kanata, the multi-media festivals Terres En Vues, and Imaginenative for supporting my movies and tolerating my antics, and many, many more that have been there throughout the years, thank you for your support.

To further wet your appetite:

Art: flickr.com/photos/chrisbose1
Music: soundcloud.com/chris-bose
Writing: findingshelter.blogspot.ca
Film: youtube.com/user/paganmannn

Images
Cover art by Bracken Hanuse Corlett
Author photo by Nicki Mackenzie

Some of these poems were previously
published: "I am a moon made of copper"
& "All I know is this," in Salish Seas: an
anthology of text + image (AWCWC,
Vancouver, 2011),"Rattles" on urban coyote
teevee (author's blog).

About Chris Bose, *Stone the Crow*:
"An important new voice on the Native
literary scene, a voice much needed, a voice
well expressed. A writer to watch."
~Tomson Highway, Kiss of the Fur Queen,
The Rez Sisters